SQUIRRELLY TALES PRESENTS

HG.

"THE WILDEST RIDE"

By

CARLA RICHARDS

ISBN: 1-4033-4378-0 (e-book)
ISBN: 1-4033-4379-9 (Paperback)

Library of Congress Number 2002108029

This book is printed on acid free paper.

Printed in the United States of America
Bloomington, IN

Illustrations by Hannah Goltz

1stBooks – rev. 08/05/02

THE WILDEST RIDE

CHAPTER ONE

Spike's legs splayed out in all four directions. His heart raced. The air whizzed past as he fell, and fell, and fell. WHAM! The ground came up to meet him and his teeth bit down hard on his tongue. "Oof!" He grunted in pain. Spike lay flat on his tummy, stunned for a moment by his fall.

Barely six weeks old, Spike's first venture alone out of the squirrel nest was supposed to be a secret. "At this rate," he muttered, "*everybody* will hear me and Mama will scold something fierce, she will, she will!"

Spike caught his breath and jumped upright, squatting on his hind legs and blinking his bright, brown eyes. He quickly looked around for GITCHA's. His Mama, Vera, had explained about GITCHA'S. All kinds of GITCHA's; Huge HUMAN-GITCHA's, HAIRY-HOUND GITCHA's and SNEAKY-CAT GITCHA's. These were three of the most dangerous.

During the last moon-time and curled up in the nest he shared with his Mama and two sisters, Veda and Vona, his mind had spun like a walnut whirl-a-gig. He wanted to discover the world outside his home. Only, Mama said no! She'd commanded, "Just wait a few more cycles of the moon, Spike. There are lots of things you should know first."

"A few more cycles," Spike complained, "and I'll be as old as a grandfather!"

Spike's ears wiggled as he listened. His head jerked this way and that, his spiky tail flicking quickly over his back as he looked wide-eyed at this new, exciting world.

Spike had only been outside the nest when he and his sisters went into the HUMAN-GITCHA's backyard with their mother. They stayed close to her, never wandering far away.

Now, he was alone. It was time to explore.

"I'm big enough and brave enough, I am, I am!" He may not have got his mother's permission, but he just *had* to go see the world.

"I'm big and brave, I am," he repeated, trying to stay strong of mind. But he worried just the same and looked for a hiding place.

Spike saw a big round thing near the side of the Human house. Tall, yellow flowers poked out of the top, waving in the breeze. Smelling something to eat, he dashed across the grass toward the flowerpot.

Food was never far from Spike's mind, especially when he felt afraid. He jumped into the center of the round thing and to his delight found dirt! He scratched beneath the large leaves of the bright flowers chattering happily.

"What are these things? What? What?" Spike sniffed at the sunflower seeds that had fallen. He picked one up and nibbled around the edges, then spit out the center, and sighed, "Ooooo! That was different!" He dug faster hoping to find the familiar acorn he smelled hiding deeper beneath the soil.

As newborn squirrels, Spike and his sisters first nursed from their Mama. She'd brought them seeds and small acorns for them to munch. He and his sisters only recently learned how to find their own food. Spike learned very quickly and enjoyed the many different seeds that fell from the bird feeder on the pole in the human's backyard.

Just as he found the nut, he heard strange and harsh sounds. HUMAN-GITCHA voices! He'd heard them before. He had even seen a human, but he'd never been this close.

They were huge, ugly GITCHA's and very dangerous, but he remembered Mama saying that they could also be kind.

Spike tucked these memories away but knew he should be careful. Curiosity won and Spike huddled beneath the flower leaves staying very still and listening.

"Come on, Jerry. Get your bike and don't forget your lunch box!"

Spike thought, *Goobeldy gop!* "Can't understand them!"

"I'm coming, Will! Where are we going today?" Jerry called out.

Spike stretched up and gripped the side of the flower pot, trembling as he watched the two Humans.

"Let's go to the park and throw rocks in the stream," said Will.

"Yeah!" replied Jerry, "and we can eat our sack lunch there, too. It'll feel just like being in the country."

Spike pulled himself up a smidgen trying to hear them better. "Pull my tail! Grunts and chirps! I can't figure it out! Wish I could speak Human or maybe they could speak Squirrel!" There was a lot he'd like to know. He thought, *I'll just wait and see what they do.*

Spike watched one of them open a bag hanging over one side of some strange looking thing and stuff something that rattled into it. Then he opened the other side, and reaching into his shirt pulled out a furry little creature that wiggled and tried to jump from his hands.

"I'm taking Jackson with me," Jerry hollered.

"Oh, no!" cried Will, "Not that stupid guinea pig! He'll get lost again and we'll never get to play."

"No, he won't. I've got a leash for him. You'll see. I'm training him to stay on this towel." Jerry waved a bright green towel over his head then stuffed it into the saddlebag.

Spike watched wide-eyed as the Human gently placed the guinea pig inside and buckled the flap closed.

"Well, okay," answered Will. "Guess we'll see what happens. But don't let him near my peanut butter and jelly sandwich! Last time, he ate half of it and I went hungry until dinner!"

The two HUMAN-GITCHA's hopped onto the two strange looking things whose round legs rolled, and disappeared around the corner, food, guinea pig and all.

What *is* *happening* *here!* Spike blinked in disbelief as he saw the human put the rodent into the saddlebag. *That* *furry* *rat* *is* *going* *on* *an* *adventure* *and* *it's* *not* *fair!* *Not* *fair!*

"Spike! Where *is* that boy?"

Spike heard his mother's voice all the way from the flowerpot.

CHAPTER TWO

"Uh oh." Spike leaped completely out of the flowerpot into the surrounding grass and bounded across the yard as fast as his legs could carry him. "I'm in trouble again, I am, I am." The grass seemed so tall that he could scarcely see above the towering blades. Insects buzzed loudly within the grassy jungle and flew above Spike's head.

"Get out of my way! Move!" Spike squeaked as he made his way to the big oak tree. He vaulted onto the trunk and circled round and round.

WHUMP! His nose smashed into a cushy chest nearly knocking him free of his grip. Shaking his head to gain vision brought forth the image of his mother, her mouth a slash of disapproval, and brown eyes glittering with anger.

"Spike. You're out of the nest without my permission. It is by The Great Gatherer's grant that you have survived this day and you can count your lucky whiskers that I don't thwack you all the way home."

"I'm sorry, Mama. Truly I am, I am. But I just had to go out on my own. The waiting is bad enough but the others taunt and tease me!"

"What others?" She questioned as she nosed him toward a large loose-leafed nest near the top of the tree.

Two little squirrels jumped into view and ran along the branches squeaking and flicking their tails.

"Oh Spiky! Precious little Spiky!" Spike's sister, Vona, dashed away out on a limb.

"Slow squirrel, spiky tail, you're in deep acorn shells!" Veda, his other sister yelled in a sing-song manner, then turned and flicked her full bushy tail.

"See!" Spike whined, "They do, and soon every squirrel in four backyards are gonna, they are, they are!"

"Girls, come to the nest right now," their mama commanded. They all made their way above. The girls cuddled into the leaves on one side while Spike settled beside his mama on the other.

"Now," she began, "This has gone on long enough. You two must stop this nonsense. Spike can't help it if his tail has not yet grown all in."

"I hate my name and I hate my tail! Why didn't ya name me after somebody, too?" Spike questioned. His sisters were named after their Grandmother, Voda.

He didn't understand why he also wasn't given a name worth clicking!

"Your name is right for you, Spike, and besides, one day you'll make a new name for yourself. Let me tell you a story."

Spike squirmed, "Awwww! Why're you gonna tell another story, Mama? Why? Why?"

"Squirrels love to tell stories, Spike. In the first place, that's how knowledge is passed from one generation to the next. This is how we learn about family histories and squirrel traditions. Besides, between frolicking, foraging and snoozing, what else have we got to do? So, you pay attention. Someday, you, too, will want to tell them."

"Go on, Mama," begged Vona.

Veda jumped up and sidled next to her, "Yes. We want to hear."

The story began, "I wanted my babies to have the right names because names are very important. They add to one's personality, and I wanted you to have all the confidence in the world.

"I named you girls after your famous grandmother, Voda. I changed the "O" to "E" for one of you and changed the "D" to an "N" for the other."

Mama Vera continued, "You," she lovingly touched her nose with the little girl's, "have always been such a sweet, quiet baby. The name, Vona, seemed just right for you." The youngster's extra long face and long, pointy nose reminded Mama Vera of Squeal Squirrel, their father.

I named you Veda," she stated, reaching over to place a paw on top of the other little squirrel's head, "because you inherited your grandmother's coloring and tail."

"Tell us the story again, please!" begged Veda and Vona.

"Yeah! Tell it again!" Spike chimed in, his reasons for wanting to hear the story were different from his sisters. He *had* to remember every detail so that his own adventure might be bigger and better.

Their mama began, "Your Grandmother Voda was a Russian Squirrel with a beautiful tail that was bushier and darker than the local squirrels. She is legendary among the neighborhood. Her story being nearly the first told to all squirrel children. Known as a hero to all, even though she was at first, scorned and teased.

"As a very young squirrel, your Grandmother Voda ventured a long, long, way, and in the most extraordinary manner. She'd lived in a country called Russia, all the way across a great ocean. A lonely human girl-child named Vera befriended her. When the little human girl learned from her mother and father that the family would leave Russia, sail on a boat clear across the world to a new country, why, the little girl couldn't bear to leave her furry friend behind!

"Come with me," she'd begged the little squirrel, "I'll bring along grass and acorns and make sure that you're safe." After great thought, Voda decided to accept the invitation to start a new life in a new country. She trusted the child would keep her safe. She hid in the little girl's backpack, and true to her promise, the child delivered her safely to a new, forest home in America.

"The gray squirrels teased her about her accent, because she chattered a little bit differently. They called her a liar when she explained how she was a friend of the human girl now living in the house at the edge of the forest. They thought she'd been hit in the head with a nut when she told about having been on a boat and ridden inside a VROOM, a car, as it is called.

"But eventually, with the help of the little girl-child, Vera, they soon believed her. She'd made friends, and because of her bushier than usual tail, she even won the Oak Day race, proving that she was a very fast running squirrel, indeed.

"When I was born, I was given the little girl's name, Vera," Mama said reverently, "and even though it's a human name, I feel very proud of it."

"But, but, what about me? How come I wasn't named after somebody special, how come, how come?" Spike questioned his mama and hopped up and down among the loose leaves of the nest.

"As I watched you scoot and root around in the nest, I tried to envision you as a grown up squirrel, bushy-tailed and smart. Your eyes were bright and you had fine little ears, but the fur on your tail—it was growing in kind of spiky. So I named you Spike. Not just because of your tail, but because you will grow up tough and smart. And don't worry, one day, yours will be the bushiest tail of them all, and you'll be the fastest running squirrel ever and one of great renown!"

Spike puffed with pride at his mama's praise.

"I'm pretty fast now, I am, I am, but, I've gotta do something special, Mama. I want to play in the Autumn Acorn Scramble and I've just gotta go explore. I've gotta do something special!"

Spike hopped and twirled and ran around the nest stepping all over his squealing sisters.

"All in good time, Spike. You are young yet and must be very careful. You must remember all my teachings and watch for GITCHA's. And most of all, you must gain my permission to go exploring, at least for a while. Promise me." Mama looked sternly at Spike and waited for his answer.

"I'll be careful, I will, I will," promised Spike.

The family of squirrels settled into the nest for the afternoon. The sun shone strong through the leaves of the tree, its warmth making the squirrels sleepy. All, that is, except Spike. His mind whirled remembering what he saw. *I've just got to have an*

19

adventure! The Autumn Acorn Scramble will happen soon, and I want to join in the fun!

Spike knew that if a young squirrel had a special talent, or could brag about a great adventure, the older squirrels might include him in spite of his age.

The Autumn Acorn Scramble allowed everyone a chance to qualify for The Oak Day Race that took place just before winter. In order to win the famous race, a squirrel had to be able to run fast enough to beat a nut falling to the ground through a leafy tree. Many acorns scattered the ground when the race was run. Only the fastest squirrels participated, and only one would win.

Going through the hole in the roof straight out of the nest was Spike's first step toward a grand adventure. It was scary to be out alone but he was determined to make a new name for himself.

Spike fretted. *Wish my tail were bushier. I could run faster if it would just grow!*

Spike nearly cried at the thought. He *hated* his tail and he *hated* his name. They were the same—SPIKY!

CHAPTER THREE

The birthing nest Spike and his sisters called

home nestled within the eaves over the porch of

the human house. The hollow area beneath the

roof made a perfect place for their den. A

tall wooden fence divided the backyards, giving

the squirrels a high place to scamper about and

spring onto low-hanging branches of the trees.

New morning light from the sunrise told the

squirrels of a new day. "Get up sleepyhead!

Get up!" Vona nudged Spike's backside with her

long nose. "It's time to eat."

Spike yawned and stretched his legs. Remembering his quest, he jumped up and started for the hole in the eaves near the fence.

"Not so fast, young sir," said his mother. "You must wash your face before you go out."

Spike griped, but set to the chore, first licking one paw and running it over an eye, then scratching rapidly at an ear with a back paw. *Good enough!*

He was the first one to spring through the hole onto the fence, making a dash toward the oak tree. There he waited while his sisters and mother caught up with him. They rooted in the grass below the bird feeder in the middle of the yard and took turns eating at the wooden box nailed to the tree. The humans living there kept it full of yummy things like corn kernels and peanuts.

Spike and his sisters played chase, never quite catching one another but chattering happily. Their mother looked on with pride. Her babies grew wittier and faster every day.

In spite of their mama's scolding yesterday, Spike's sisters teased him, "Spiky, your tail's growing in spiky."

"Stop it, I say!" Spike stomped his feet and whisked his tail.

"Maybe we'll call you *"Precious,"* giggled Vona.

"What a lovely boy you are," laughed Veda. "Look how *precious* your fur is!"

Vona ran in a circle around Spike and taunted, "Yes! Come give us a hug, *Precious!*"

"Don't call me that! Besides, you're just stupid tree rats and can't run." He hated when his sisters teased.

Spike kicked at the fallen acorns, showering his sisters with the hard nuts. The two girls laughed so hard they rolled around in the grass, not realizing how their actions and name-calling hurt Spike's feelings. They just thought that *"Precious"* was a funny thing to call their brother.

"Girls! Girls!" Mama called to her daughters. "Stop teasing your brother. I'm disappointed in you!"

When they heard their mother's scolding, Veda and Vona stopped, their little ears flattened with shame.

"We're sorry, Mama," they said together.

Their mother shook a paw at them, "Don't apologize to me. Say you're sorry to your brother."

"Do we have to?" Veda and Vona whined.

"Anyway, he started it. He called us tree rats and kicked nuts at us!"

"Girls!" Vera frowned. "Don't blame Spike. You're the ones calling him names. You chose to act the way you did. You have to be responsible for your own actions and accept the consequences."

"And—Spike." She spoke sternly. "I'm ashamed of you, too. We're supposed to take care of one another, not be hurtful."

"But they weren't being nice to me. It's not fair- not fair!" He turned his head so his mama couldn't see him and stuck out his tongue at his sisters. They crossed their eyes at him then turned and twitched their bushier tails.

"Alright, children. That's quite enough. It's time to eat. Come with me, girls." Mama and the two sisters grazed around the yard munching on seeds and nuts the birds flung about from the bird feeder on the pole. Spike managed a turn at the wooden squirrel feeder box nailed to the large oak tree, content to appear separate from his family.

Their stomachs full from breakfast, Spike's sisters and mother climbed up high in the tree for a rest. Spike found a comfortable spot on a branch and sprawled out flat, his eyes staring across the space of his home yard.

As the sun rose higher in the sky, an idea came to him and he jumped up, looking at his mother resting on a branch high above. *She won't know as long as I'm quiet and fast*, he thought, forgetting his earlier promise to gain permission before venturing away.

Spike scrambled to the edge of the tree limb and leaped onto the fence. "I'm going to see what's in that yard," he mumbled. He peered into the neighboring yard and noticed two or three other squirrels grazing in the grass on the far side.

"Hey! Anything good over there?" Spike chattered.

The other squirrels raised their heads and looked at him. "Pretty good nibblin's. C'mon over and get some!"

"Be strong of mind—strong of mind," Spike mumbled, working up his courage.

Jumping off the fence and springing through the grass, Spike worked his way toward the other squirrels, digging into the sprigs of grass as he went.

KREE-E-E-E! KREE-E-E-E! The pig-like squeal echoed from high above. A shadow

crossed the yard at the same time. *What's that?*
Spike jumped and looked up at the sky.

"KUK, KUK, HAWK!" The other squirrels
yelled as they ran toward the tree for cover.
"Run for your life!"

A hawk sailed into view and took up station.
The black-edged tip of its tail bent down and
pointed wings beat rapidly as it searched the
ground below.

Spike froze with fear. He could not move
and hunkered down among the blades of grass,
his eyes closed. He cried, "What do I do?
What? What?"

As the bird turned and slid sideways and
downward, Spike's mother commanded from the
fence. "Spike! Run! Hide in the tree!"

The shadow of the hawk crossed over Spike.
As the bird came lower in an oblique glide,
dropping with wings closed, Spike heard its cry
and knew his life was over.

Instinct told him this giant bird would
carry him away, away from his mother and his

troublesome sisters, and away from his safe home. He would never have a great adventure, practice in the Autumn Acorn Scramble or race on Oak Day. He would just be this bird's dinner.

"Spike! Use your tail, son! Run fast to the tree!" Spike heard his mother's voice on the wind and turning, saw her spring off the fence toward him. Seeing his mother spurred him to movement.

Spike jumped and his little feet moved beneath him, carrying him toward the tree. He heard the hawk's rasping scream and knew the bird was near.

"I'm gonna gitcha! I'm gonna gitcha!" The bird screeched and dived down toward the little squirrel.

Spike flicked his tail hard and leaped toward the trunk of the tree, his mother just behind him. They both circled around and around the trunk, up and up they went, the leaves of the oak tree hampering the hawk's mission.

The hawk turned at the last moment, swooping high into the sky. "Next time, little squirrel. I'll gitcha next time."

"No!" Spike screamed. His experience with the hawk disturbed his sleep for the second night in a row. His mama patted his head and soothed him back to sleep. During the day, he kept closer to the tree and his mother.

That's the only adventure I'll ever have. I am too much of a coward to try for another! Spike lamented. His legs trembled in fear as he remembered how close he came to his life's end. If the hawk had been successful he would have been carried away, never to see his mother and sisters again.

"But this *can't* be all there is," he mumbled, ashamed that he wasn't the brave squirrel he thought himself to be. "It just can't!"

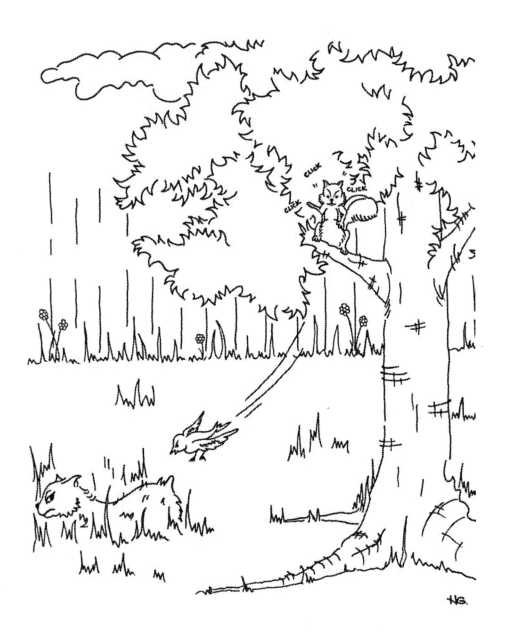

CHAPTER FOUR

"I'm going to tell you a story about a wily CAT-GITCHA named No-Tail," Spike's mama announced.

After his experience with the hawk, Spike was not allowed out of her sight and to tell the truth, he was glad, for the moment. Even though his greatest desire was to prove himself by having a special adventure to share, he knew he had a lot to learn.

His Mama loved to act out stories. His sisters, Veda and Vona, enjoyed their mama's play-acting. Spike thought it rather silly,

34

but at least with the learning made fun, it helped them remember things.

"Before you were born, I had to find a place to build my special nest, one where you would be safe.

"I searched everywhere. First I looked in an Elm tree in one yard, but as it was still early spring, it didn't have enough leaves for cover."

Mama held a paw above her eyes, pretending to look far and wide.

"I hopped onto a very tall wooden fence, yes," she whisked her tail in the direction of the fence, "that one over there, and up on the low-hanging branches of this very tree. A live oak tree keeps its leaves all year round and provides lots of camouflage. But it was already occupied by at least two other squirrel families. I tried several trees in other yards, but they were all taken. I even tried the tree with the large hole in the trunk where I keep extra nuts and goodies, but there was no room for a birthing nest in the same tree. Things looked grim, indeed.

"Then, just as I was about to give up all hope, I discovered a hole in the roof of the porch of the human house. Human houses make wonderful squirrel mansions for those Gatherers brave enough to live near the HUMAN-GITCHA's."

Spike imagined his Mama pouncing through the grass, happy and excited to have found a home at last.

She continued, "My brain busy with all I needed to do, I didn't notice danger creeping toward me.

"From the sky, a jay-bird named Blue screeched a warning. "There! In the grass," he screeched. "A fat CAT-GITCHA!"

"Not only that," sneered Mama, "It was an ugly, gray and black cat with its tail missing!"

Spike watched as Mama acted out the part of the ugly, dangerous CAT-GITCHA. "Well, I thought, must not be a very good cat to have lost its tail! But cats are very dangerous, with or without a tail.

"The minute I started moving I knew No-Tail would be after me. That mean, sneaky CAT-GITCHA crouched between a safe tree and me. No-Tail let out a heart-stopping hunting howl then leaped to a run!"

Spike shivered. He could imagine that howl, and, in fact, had heard them screeching in the night below the nest.

"YIKES! I yelled when another sound came from nearby. *That* scared me even more, but I didn't dare stop to see what it was. No-Tail was right behind me! I could almost feel his breath on my fur!" Mama showed Spike and his sisters how to spring into action and run like the wind, as she had that day.

"Go on, Mama," urged Spike, "What happened, then?"

"Just as I reached the tree, a huge paw clamped down on the end of my tail!

"GOTCHA! No-Tail yowled."

Spike shuddered, watching his Mama's eyes twitch while she told that part, no doubt remembering her own fear.

"I dug my feet into the ground and leaped as hard and high as I could. My tail slipped free of the cat's grasp. I circled the tree and sprang from branch to branch until I reached the highest limb.

"Expecting No-Tail to be right behind me, I turned to fight. Was I surprised," she exclaimed. "No-Tail was slinking through the grass toward the shrubs, howling in anger. Blue, the jaybird screeched past, diving and pecking at that stupid cat's head! I thanked Blue and promised to return the favor someday. It pays to be friendly with other creatures," Mama said. "You never know when you might need a friend."

"Wow!" All three of the young squirrels hopped wide-eyed around their mother.

"Is No-Tail still around, Mama?" Spike wanted to know. If he planned on being out alone, he wanted to know to watch for this particular cat. If it almost got his mama, it might get him, too.

"I've seen him a time or two, but all cats are dangerous, Spike, one of the most dangerous GITCHA'S that live! You have to look in every direction for them for they are wily indeed."

CHAPTER FIVE

The fourth day after Spike's scary experience with the hawk dawned bright and sunny. Dewy grass sparkled in the morning sun. Spike, his mother and sisters left the nest. They ate seeds thrown on the ground by Blue and his other feathered friends, and licked the wet blades of grass. It was a beautiful morning, peaceful in the first light of day and creatures of all kinds broke the silence with their happy voices.

"Today," vowed Spike, "I will be brave. I will seek a new adventure. I will have strength of mind, I will, I will." He moved farther from the tree and the other Gatherers, determined to find his own way.

Nearly half way across the yard Spike heard familiar HUMAN-GITCHA voices intruding on the quiet scene. He sprinted to the wooden fence closest to him and sat still watching them and tried to understand their sounds.

"I love Saturdays," said Jerry as he opened the side door to the garage.

"Me, too. Especially when I sleep over at your house."

"Let's head for the field. We can play super heroes!"

Will and Jerry closed the garage door, mounted their bicycles and rode away from the house.

Spike watched as the boys disappeared, just as they had the first day. Even though he was frightened, he wasn't as afraid of the humans as he had been of the hawk. An idea began to form in his mind.

"I've only got a short time left," he told himself. "The Autumn Acorn Scramble will happen soon, and I've just *got* to have something to brag about. The big squirrels will let me practice with them if I've had a great adventure."

Little by little, Spike sprang through the grass toward the opening from where the humans had come. Not far from the door sat the round thing with the tall yellow flowers, and beyond that was another shorter fence. Spike turned and noticed his mother still dozing on a tree branch. His sisters were nowhere in sight. Bothersome girls!

He looked at the short fence between the two human dwellings and with more bravery than he felt, dashed toward it, hopped on to the top and plunged into the grass on the other side. Spike stayed very still in the way squirrels do. He'd never gone to the other side of the fence before.

His bright brown eyes took in the different sights expanding his world.

"What was that?" he clicked. A huge noisy creature whizzed past, then quickly disappeared down a stretch of gray ground. Spike could not understand it! He looked around for a place to hide. Trembling but curious, he backed up and huddled near the fence trying to blend into the colorful flowers growing there. From this safe distance, he watched another beast go by. Spike was amazed.

He caught a glimpse of another squirrel from the neighborhood hopping from branch to branch of a nearby tree. He decided to make a run for it. *Surely,* he thought, *I'll be safe in the tree.*

Glassy-eyed and staring at the tree, he remembered his mama's words; a lesson handed down from his famous grandmother Voda.

"Everything is energy. All the people, all the creatures, all things are energy. Think the energy into yourself and store it in your mind and your body."

His Grandmother Voda's theory that every being was linked together and created energy had sounded pretty silly, but Spike was willing to try it. If he just imagined the outcome the way he wanted it to be, it would become so. Because he could see it in his mind, could picture himself already in the tree, he would be safe.

Spike stared hard at the tree. He saw himself safely high on a limb, the sun shining down on his fur, the breeze blowing softly through the trees.

Taking a deep breath, he glanced around for GITCHA's, dug in his feet and flicking his tail sprinted quickly to the tree.

"Whew! It worked! I made it, I did. I did." Spike gasped as he scampered to a limb near the top and sprawled flat to disguise his presence.

"Hey, you, KOO-KOO."

Spike looked around for the voice.

"Yeah! KOO-KOO. You there, sprawled on that fat limb. Whatcha think you're doin' in this tree. This 'un's mine, don't ya know."

Spying the large bird perched on a limb not far from him caused Spike alarm. His experience with the hawk still fresh in his mind, he wasn't sure this one was friend or foe.

"S-s-s-sorry, bird," Spike stuttered and sat upright.

"Bird! Name's Pudger. I'm a pigeon, don'tcha know?"

"S-s-s-sorry, Mr. Pigeon, er, Pudger. I was just getting out of harm's way. I've never been this side of the fence before and I'm looking for adventure."

"Well, by covey! I think you'll find it! Lots of goings-on over here," replied the pigeon. The speckled bird ruffled its feathers.

"What are those fast things down there on the gray ground." Spike was very curious.

"VROOMS! Don'tcha know? Humans call 'em Cars. Hey, here comes one now. Watch!" The plump bird hopped forward on the branch to get a better view.

Spike balanced on hind legs, stretched his neck, and watched as the loud beast zoomed past.

"Wow! That monster is fast!"

"Sure are," cooed the pigeon, "This way and that—up and down. Vroom and zoom! Keeps me from nappin' they do, KOO-KOO."

"Don't they ever sleep?"

"Sure do, KOO-KOO," replied Pudger. "And that's when I get my revenge. When they're not moving, I walk on them and leave droppings as gifts. Makes the human's mad, but by then I've flown the coop! KOO-HA!" The bird chuckled and flapped his wings.

Spike joined the big bird in laughter. The sun moved to hide behind a house across the road and Spike felt he had stayed long enough. Saying goodbye, he scampered down the tree and

47

scrambled back over the short fence to the back yard. *I'll come back tomorrow*, thought Spike, *and explore.*

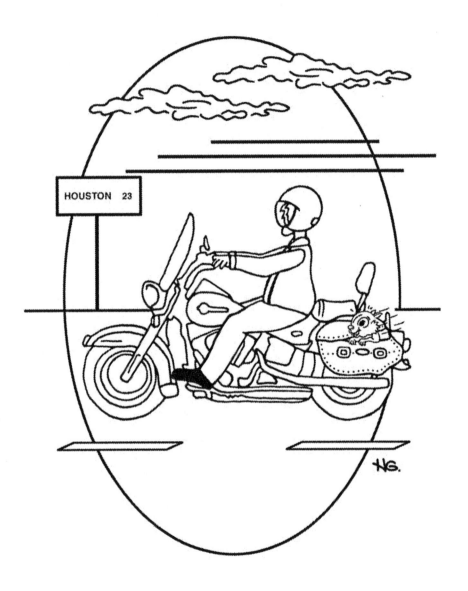

CHAPTER SIX

Just as the sun was rising, Spike scooted out
of the nest and headed toward the front yard.
He dashed across the grass, scampered over the
short fence he'd crossed the day before, and
leaped onto the pigeon's tree. There, he
waited and watched. He didn't know what he was
watching for, but as in the way of squirrels,
observed the rest of nature as the sun turned
the sky pink.

A door to the people house opened and a
large human came through. The tall human
stretched his arms over his head and yawned.

Spike remembered his mother's description of Man, and decided that this must be one. He was much larger than the other two he'd observed the past few days. Spike watched as the man walked to a large creature and removed a great white cover.

Spike frantically wondered, *"Is that the Thing's skin? What's he doing? What? What?"* The Thing whose skin was removed didn't seem to mind, so Spike decided that maybe it wasn't a living creature after all. When the covering was completely off, Spike blinked his eyes as the sun bounced off the thing. The creature was black and shiny and had two round feet! It reminded him of the rolling things that the two smaller humans disappeared on. But it was much bigger. He remembered Jackson, the rodent, and how he rode in a bag on the rolling thing and went away with the smaller humans.

He watched curiously as the man stuffed the cover into a large bag hanging over the back leaving the flap open. Turning, the man went back into the people house.

Spike carefully moved down the trunk of the tree and onto the grass below. Looking about, Spike did not see anyone, so he slowly hopped nearer.

Should I? He debated. *Mama will be upset, but here's my chance for adventure!* With no more thought, Spike scampered toward the Thing and leaped onto the outside of the bag. He stopped only to catch his breath and look around for GITCHA's. He climbed to the top and slipped into the opening, burrowing down into the skin shoved into the deep, dark bag. He tried to be still but was so scared his whole body trembled.

"Oh! What have I done?" he clicked quietly. He was amazed at his bravery, astounded by his courage, awed by his daring! By gosh, here was high adventure! Spike was sure no squirrel had ever been inside the skin of a huge monster like this before!

"I'll stay just a minute, then I'll climb out and go home," Spike vowed, rooting around inside the bag.

All of a sudden, Spike's whole world rocked! The Thing with two round feet bounced up and down and teetered from side to side. A human hand came down almost on top of him closing the flap. His world became dark as night.

"Whoa!" clicked Spike, "What's happening! What? What?"

BRRROOOOM! BRRROOOOM! The *Thing* screamed! It sounded like hundreds of angry bees flying around in his head! Spike covered his ears against the noise. Burrowing deeper into the skin was the only thing he could think to do.

The angry bee sound changed and softened slightly. He felt his space tilt first one way and then another. Peeking through his claws he could see a tiny bit of light showing through the top of the bag. Bravely, Spike uncurled his little body and pushing with his tail climbed slowly toward the top. When he reached the opening he poked his head through the small hole.

"YIKES!" he screamed and ducked his head. "Be strong of mind—strong of mind." He chattered quietly and slowly edged his head through the hole once more. The Thing was running with him in it! People houses whizzed by and trees blurred as they passed. A VROOM going the opposite way came so close Spike was sure he would be flattened.

Gripping the bag firmly with his claws, he pushed his way up in order to see better. His eyes blinked in the wind as he watched the world go by with astounding speed.

"Hey! This is really sweet!" Spike chattered and clicked, his fear nearly forgotten. His big two front teeth showed as his lips curled into the biggest grin a squirrel ever had.

"Look at me!" he yelled, "I'm flying like a bird, I am, I am!" In spite of his excitement, Spike carefully and curiously watched the human in front of him. He wondered if this one was a GITCHA. He worried about being seen by the man and kept his legs beneath him, ready to burrow back down into the bag at a moment's notice.

The sun rose higher in the sky. The Thing still ran taking him farther away from home. He thought of his mother and sisters, and his friends in the neighboring yard, and began to really worry.

Will I ever see home again? He thought about his Grandmother Voda and the story about how she'd left her home, never to see her family and friends again. *Am I going to a different country like Grandmother?*

The buzz of the round-footed Thing changed again, slowed, then came to a halt. The man in front of Spike put his feet on the ground and the loud bee sound quit. Spike scrambled into the bag out of sight. A long time passed.

When Spike was sure the human had left, he bravely crawled toward the opening.

Gripping the top of the bag he pulled himself through the small hole and looked around. All he could see was the gray ground and far across the way was a small bit of grass and two trees. The sun beat down making the top of his head hot. He wasn't used to being directly in the sun for long periods of time. All squirrels seek the shade of their nests during the day to sleep and stay out of the summer sun.

"What should I do? What? What?" Spike clicked, "How can I get home?" Sadly, he crawled down into the bag. It was cooler at the bottom away from the sun's rays, and even though he couldn't breathe very well, his instincts told him to stay in the bag.

Spike slept and in his dream, the big yellow flower in the flowerpot smelled wonderful. The seeds below the bird feeder in his yard tasted so moist he licked his lips in his sleep. The acorns from the great oak tree crunched between his teeth. Spike's stomach growled waking him.

Where is that Man! He wished the human would come back and take him home. He was hot, hungry, thirsty, and very scared. He didn't know how his grandmother could have stayed hidden on a boat so long, away from the comforting trees and sweet grass. He sighed, feeling very sad. His great adventure had turned into a horrible nightmare.

Spike decided to venture outside the bag. He poked his little head out of the hole and looked around. He was alone. He quickly popped the rest of his body out of the hole and with his spiky tail, leaped from the bag onto the gray ground beside the rolling Thing.

With the breeze he smelled the bark of the trees and the green grass. "Trees!" Spike squeaked and dashed toward them, but stopped in the middle of the road. He'd never crossed gray ground before and stood up on his hind legs to get a better look. The gritty surface felt hot from the sun nearly causing him to hop from paw to paw. The ground rumbled and a loud noise filled his ears.

A huge yellow VROOM came toward him with great speed. He had only a moment to decide which way to turn; toward the trees or back to the rolling Thing. Nearly upon him, the VROOM screeched at him! Spike pushed forward with his tail and ran as fast as he could toward the green grass. He leaped onto the first tree he came to.

"Whew! I made it!" His breath whooshed from his lungs, his heart pitter-patting rapidly. He perched round-eyed on a limb looking about.

Spike rested a moment or two. His tummy growled and he decided to look for food. He munched wild seeds found in the grass, which were very tasty. The tree offered pecans, a sweet nut Spike had not tasted before.

"Ooooo, this is delicious!" Spike happily sighed, eating until he was stuffed. He gazed toward the running thing that had brought him here and watched for the man. His day had been very exciting. With his tummy full and the sun warm, Spike grew sleepy. He stretched out on a branch of the pecan tree and fell sound asleep.

BRRROOOOM … BRRROOOOM! The familiar noise awoke Spike! He sat up and rubbed the sleep from his eyes and gazed toward the sound.

"The man! The man is leaving! Oh, no-o-o!" He jumped completely off the tree and without looking, bounded to the center of the road. He chased after the racing Thing, but it was just too fast. Breathless, he stopped, sat back on his rump and watched sadly as he was left behind.

CHAPTER SEVEN

"Now what do I do?" Spike wailed. A big tear rolled from his eye wetting the fur on his face.

The gray ground rumbled as another VROOM came towards him. Several more started moving about, spurring the little squirrel to get off the road. He sprinted toward the grass and the safety of the pecan trees, barely getting out of the way of the VROOMS.

The sun dipped low on the horizon, darkness not far behind. Spike gnawed on pecans until his tummy ached then went from branch to branch trying to find a comfortable spot to sleep until morning. *I'll think about what to do later. I'm too tired now.*

"Are there any squirrels around here? Hulloo!" he called out loud, "Any friendly birds about?" He appeared to be the only creature around and to tell the truth, he was a tiny bit afraid of the dark.

In his neighborhood, other creatures usually lounged about until well after dark, but here, he seemed alone. *Some adventure this is.* Grumpily, Spike turned around on a fat limb and sprawled out flat, staring across the expanse of gray ground.

He recalled his Mama's face, and how she would pull him close to her at the end of day. He thought of the stories she told about their grandmother's great adventure. He grinned, remembering his sisters and how they called him 'Precious' and teased him about his spiky tail. He would miss them, he decided, he would miss them all.

"HISS-S-S-S-S! HISS-S-S-S-S! Whatcha doin'
here! Get out of my tree!"

Spike blinked his eyes at a creature hanging
upside down by its tail! "Who's that! Who?
Who?" Spike asked anxiously, "What are you?
Why is this *your* tree?" He stumbled backward
on the branch away from the creature.

"Just never you mind what I am. But if you
must know, my name is Go-Away Possum. Now get
out of my tree!" The opossum hissed and bared
her teeth.

Spike bravely faced the creature but trusted
her not at all. "I can't leave right now, not
until I think how. I've had a great adventure,
you see, and now I have to find my way home."

Go-Away Possum thought for a moment, "How'd
you get here then, fly?"

Spike laughed a little, "Almost. I rode in
this rolling Thing with two round feet. I've

come a long way. The Man that lives in the People house where our nest is brought me, only ... he left without me and now, I don't know how to get home, I don't, I don't." Spike tried to sound brave but his bottom lip quivered with sadness.

Go-Away Possum swung herself upright on the tree and stared at Spike, her pink eyes shining in the dark. "That don't make sense. Never heard of a Human bringing a squirrel out here and dropping him off. Kittens maybe, but not squirrels."

"Well, he did. He didn't know I was hiding inside the round-footed thing and now, I'm stuck. So, I've got to stay right here in this tree until I can think what to do."

Go-Away Possum scrunched her pink nose in thought, then asked, "Have you been out here all day?"

"Long enough for me to nearly die of the heat stuffed in a bag on the running thing. I got hungry and thought I'd find something to eat and before I knew it, he left without me, he did, he did." Spike jumped back as Go-Away Possum gripped the tree limb with her tail and threw her body off the branch. The creature swung back and forth by her tail, and said nothing for a long time.

"Hum-m-m-m-m. Go back to sleep, squirrel. I'm thinking," she ordered in her gritty voice.

Spike moved to another branch and left the opossum alone. She was a strange creature and rather frightening.

The crickets chirped a night song and in spite of the strange, swinging opossum, Spike dozed off.

"Hey Squirrel." THUMP. THUMP. The opossum's tail made Spike's branch tremble.

"What? What?" Spike jumped as the loud noise on the branch awoke him. "Go-Away,

Possum," he demanded, "I was sleeping like you told me to." Grumpily, Spike scratched and backed away from the smelly thing. Go-Away Possum thumped her tail again on Spike's branch. Spike jumped out of the way.

"Yup. That's my name," the creature replied. "Well, if you'd put your noggin to good use, seems to me you'd find a solution. But, since you're not thinking, it's up to me."

"Now see here, madam," began Spike feeling insulted, but the bossy Possum took charge.

"Here's what I know, so listen and learn, little lunchkin." Spike wondered had he been a younger squirrel, if, indeed, he would have been lunch for Go-Away Possum. Here was a new kind of GITCHA, one that looked safe but wasn't.

"Here's the deal," Go-Away Possum said, "If that Human came here once, he'll probably come again, and when that happens you cross the gray ground and climb back inside the *Thing*, and see where you end up."

"Do you really think he'll come back? Do you? Do you?" Spike hopped up and down excitedly.

The creature told him the plan. "You watch in the morning when all the Humans come back. They'll stop their running things over there in that big gray square. Most of the same ones come here every day and leave every night. They leave trash over there," she motioned toward a barrel, "and that's where I get my eats."

"Thanks. I'll do that." Spike felt excited about the possibility of his human coming back. The sky began to turn pink as the sun peeked over the horizon. He'd had enough sleep and decided to practice leaping from tree to tree. The smaller limbs weren't as sturdy as the larger limbs, but it was fun to risk falling. Spike loved the thrill.

Birds flew overhead, their morning cries heard from high above. The creature from the night disappeared. Spike wondered where she'd gone. He'd never really properly thanked her. His mother would have been disappointed in his lack of manners.

VROOMS sped past the small grassy area with the pecan trees. Spike watched with interest as the running things sped past, but they were all wrong. They had four round feet instead of two and none stopped and stayed put as they had the day before.

Maybe Go-Away Possum was wrong. Maybe Spike would never see the man again. Maybe, he would become a roaming squirrel, one that never quite fit in with others.

Squirrels almost always live their lives near their birth nest, never wandering far.

Only squirrels of great legend looked for adventure, like his Grandmother Voda, and now, Spike.

Darkness fell once again and for the second night, Spike found himself in the strange company of Go-Away Possum. She made her rounds of the trash barrels finding her own dinner and settled on the same limb, swinging upside down, pink eyes glaring into the night.

"The man didn't come back, Go-Away!" Spike cried. "What am I gonna do? Huh? Huh? I'm forever lost and all because I wanted to brag!"

"Just be patient and wait. Sometimes it takes two or three moon cycles for 'em to come back." Spike thanked her for her counsel but wondered if she really knew the truth. Spike found a fat limb to sleep on far away from the creature.

Guess I'll have to wait. If the man doesn't come tomorrow, I'll have to be brave and go my own way. Spike just knew he was lost forever and cried himself to sleep.

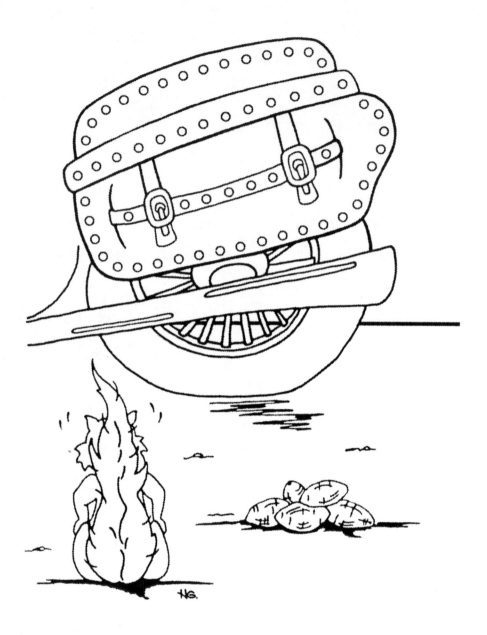

CHAPTER EIGHT

BRRROOOOM! BRRROOOOM!

Spike jumped as a black, round-footed running Thing pulled around the corner. It stopped in the same spot where it sat two days before. Spike chattered excitedly and leaped from the tree. Just as Go-Away Possum suggested, his man had returned. Spike could almost have kissed her had she not been so stinky.

Spike didn't dare cross the gray ground right now as there were too many VROOMS going this way and that. The man disappeared into the large building at the far side of the gray ground.

"He's not leaving me again," Spike vowed. All day he watched and waited. Deciding to take a few of the delicious pecans back to his family, Spike carefully crossed the gray ground many times, piling them next to the thing.

When the sun dipped lower in the sky, he crossed to the shiny black Thing and jumped onto the side of the bag clawing his way to the top.

"Oh, n-o-o-o-o!" Spike nearly cried. He couldn't get into the bag! The flap was tied down. He tried digging at it, and when that didn't work, he used his teeth and chewed and chewed until a hole formed, then he chewed some more.

"I'll get into that bag if it's the last thing I do! I will, I will!" Spike vowed. The hole at the top of the bag was finally large enough for him to slip through. He made several trips in and out carrying pecans to the bottom.

Deciding he'd collected enough, Spike curled up between the folds of the skin. "I'm going home, I am, I am." And in spite of the heat within the bag, he dozed and waited.

An ear-splitting roar startled Spike awake. He felt the Thing rumble. His world tilted as it took off. Spike scrambled to the top and poked his head out of the hole.

The wind felt cool and wonderful. It blew his fur straight back from his tiny head and he sighed with relief. Spike grinned as the world raced by. This was the best part of his great adventure.

As time went by, Spike wondered how much longer it would be until they stopped again. His eyes felt dry after staring hard into the wind and watching things go by so fast he could not tell what he was seeing. He recognized trees, of course, and people houses, but the rest of what he saw was unfamiliar. Spike got used to the buzz of the round-footed Thing and knew when it was going to slow down or go fast.

After a time, the familiar bee sound softened and Spike felt the Thing slow down. He recognized the tree from where Pudger Pigeon pooped on VROOMS. He saw the short fence he had scampered over when his big adventure began. *I'm HOME! HURRAY!* Spike thought.

The rumble of the Thing stopped and Spike scrambled down in the bag to hide. The man, he was sure, would go back into the people house. Soon, he could gather his pecans and scamper home to the nest. Spike was excited and happy. *I'll be a hero!* He couldn't wait to tell his friends and family about his wild ride. He was sure he'd be allowed to practice at the Autumn Acorn Scramble and maybe even run the Oak Day Race!

A bright stream of sunlight blinded him as the top of the bag opened and a large human hand grabbed hold of the skin. Spike hung on. Up and up he was carried with the skin out of the bag, then - WHOOSH! His claws hurt from holding on so he let go. His eyes wide with shock, he saw the sky spin, and a tree pass by turned on its side, and then gray ground came up to meet him. WHAM!

"Ouch!" Spike landed upside down on his head. He quickly righted himself and scooting on his belly, hid beneath the skin spread on the ground. Spike panted anxiously.

"Great nuts! What am I going to do? What! What!" Spike was really scared and confused. His head hurt and he wanted to go home.

"Hey! What's this?" The man exclaimed. "A young squirrel! Where'd you come from little furry fellow?"

Spike shuddered as the huge man leaned over him. He wanted to run away but his legs wouldn't work.

"Lucy! Lucy! Come here, quick!" The man hollered as he stood with hands on his hips towering over Spike.

Spike carefully backed up trying to get beneath the white tarp. His teeth chattered with fear and his fur shook in a constant tremble.

"Don't be afraid." The man said. Not waiting for Lucy, he pulled a small towel out of the bag. He shook it and approached the shuddering squirrel. "I know where I'll put you," he said.

Spike hid his head under his front paws and felt the towel cover him completely. The man was picking him up!

"DON'T TOUCH ME! DON'T TOUCH ME!" Spike screeched with alarm, struggling mightily while trying to bite the towel.

His mother had warned that humans had an awful smell about them that was different from other creatures. If it got on you, other squirrels would have nothing to do with you.

Spike couldn't imagine not ever having another friend. Maybe his family would not let him come back! To be alone might be the worse thing to happen to a squirrel, except maybe getting run over by VROOMS. No matter what happened, human touch was to be avoided at all costs.

Spike struggled against the roughness of the towel hoping to get away from the smelly man. His nostrils flared with the scent and he thought - Man did stink!

The huge hand clasped him tightly but only the towel touched him. His little head poked out of the top. The man's face was close to Spike's—too close. Spike swallowed hard, his eyes blinking, knowing there was nothing he could do. He was caught and could not escape the man's grasp.

Spike quivered, and looking the man right in the eyes warned, "Let me go, Human, or I will bite you." He stayed very still, narrowed his little brown eyes and tried to look mean.

The man chuckled and was not the least bit afraid. He turned Spike this way and that to see him better.

"You're so cute. How and when did you get into my saddle bag?" The man grinned.

Spike could not understand a thing the man garbled. And *this* human's teeth were huge! He was a lot bigger than the other two humans he'd seen. *What am I to do? What? What?* Spike squirmed and twisted, trying to bite the towel, or better yet, the man! There was no hope! He was trapped!

"I hope you've learned a lesson, little guy. Riding on motorcycles isn't for squirrels!"

The man held Spike firmly in the towel and pushing open the gate to the short fence, walked toward the oak tree in the back yard.

Spike watched, eyes squinted, his heart beating rapidly. *Where is he taking me?* Spike wondered. When he noticed the feeder tree looming above him, his heart leaped! Is *the man letting me go?*

"Here you are, little fellow. Maybe you'll get along better back here." The man carefully laid the towel with Spike in it on the ground beside the tree trunk and stepped back.

After a moment, Spike realized the man no longer held him and decided to escape while he still could.

"MAMA!" Spike screeched at the top of his lungs. "MAMA!" He circled the tree trunk around and around until he was as high as he could get. Shivering among the leaves, he watched the man below pick up the towel and walk away.

CHAPTER NINE

"Spike!" His mother's voice rang out from the top of the fence. Spike watched as his mother and sisters came toward him with alarming speed. They jumped from the fence to the tree.

"Uh-oh." Spike stayed on the topmost branch and waited. His mother sounded furious and he could hear his sisters laughing. Coming face to face with his angrily clicking mother did little to dispel the fear still within Spike. He reminded himself, "Be strong of mind—strong of mind."

His mother stopped in front of him twitching her tail with anger. Just as Spike thought she was about to give his ears a good boxing, she gathered him into her arms and hugged him, rubbing her nose across his to make sure he truly was safe. After Spike stopped shaking and his sisters stopped teasing him, his mama stood over him, crossed her arms and tapped a paw on the tree limb.

"Where have you been, Spike? I have been looking for you for two moon cycles! I thought the cat, No-Tail, might have got you, or perhaps that big dog two yards down. I want the whole tale."

"I have had the wildest ride of any squirrel anywhere!" Spike began and told his story from beginning to end. His sisters taunted him and called him a fibber. Mama hushed them several times. By the time he was through, his mama appeared thoughtful.

"So you see," said Spike, "I may not have been named after her, but I'm an adventurer just like Grandmother Voda, only better!"

Mama sighed heavily and shook her head. "That's quite a story, Spike, but I was very worried! I told you to gain my permission before you decided to go exploring. You might not have returned and we would never know what happened to you.

"Your grandmother Voda wasn't looking for adventure. She didn't just go off on some fur-ruffling ride. She wanted a better life, and she had a lot of help."

"Well, I made it back, didn't I? And now, I can brag about it to the other squirrels. And even though my tail is spiky, even though I'm still small, and even though I'm not the fastest runner, they will let me practice in the Autumn Acorn Scramble and race on Oak Day!"

Mama chuckled at her son's bragging, "Spike, you're the only squirrel I've heard of that's ever ridden away on a motorcycle."

Spike asked, "Is *that* what the rolling Thing with two round feet is called?"

"Yes, that's what Humans call it and you're one very lucky squirrel to have found your way back," his mother exclaimed. "You can thank the Great Gatherer for your blessings!"

Spike cried and hugged his mother. "And I'm glad, too! Being away and lost, I realized how important my family is to me. And even though I may go looking for adventure, I'll always love you, Mama."

Jealous, his sister, Vona, teased, "I still think you made the whole thing up 'cause Grandmother Voda rode in a VROOM."

"Yeah, you're fibbing! You're just trying to one-up her!" sneered Veda.

"Am not! Am not! You wait and see. I'll prove it!" Spike said, taking the bait. *My only hope is to go back and get those special sweet nuts!* "C'mon! I'll show you if you're brave enough!"

Spike and his sisters raced down the tree and across the grass to the short fence.

"Wait, Spike! You don't have to prove anything. Stop!" cried his mother as she raced after them.

His sisters hesitated to follow Spike over the short fence to the front yard. Spike teased them until they carefully scampered over. The three little squirrels hid beneath the flowers alongside the fence watching for any GITCHA's. Their mother appeared next to them and waited to see what Spike would do. She called to him, "Be careful, Spike."

"Okay, Mama. Stay here and watch," said Spike. Bravely, he pounced toward the motorcycle and leaped onto the bag hanging over the side. He groaned as he noticed that the man had stuffed the covering back into it. That made the pecans harder to get.

Spike smartly twitched his spiky tail at his sisters in spite of feeling a little bit scared. He clicked, reminding himself, "Be strong of mind—strong of mind."

"Show off!" Veda and Vona chattered and flicked their tails.

"Spike, Come down now." Mama begged, her voice filled with concern.

Spike disappeared into the bag and a moment later came up with a whole pecan. He held it up in his paws for their inspection and clicked, "See, here's my proof! A sweet nut we've never seen in our yard before."

He tossed the nut in the grass toward his family where it wobbled and rolled near them. They hopped forward and sniffed the delicious smelling nut, then looked at Spike in awe.

"He really did ride with the human," Vona exclaimed with excitement.

Veda watched Spike scurry down into the bag and emerge with another nut. "Yes, and look! He's bringing up another special nut!"

"I don't believe Spike's tail will make a difference, girls," Mama said proudly, "This just proves that you can't judge a squirrel by his tail. Now he'll be known far and wide as the squirrel who took the wildest ride!"

Veda pouted, knowing Spike's fame would come close to their famous grandmother's. He really could claim the wildest ride!

Just then, the door to the People house opened and the man came out. There was no time for Spike to scramble off the bag to safety so he did the next best thing. He jumped back in.

"I'm going to the store, Lucy. I'll be back later," said the man as he climbed onto the seat of the motorcycle.

BRRROOOOM! BRRROOOOM!

The shiny round-footed Thing roared as it raced out of the driveway and disappeared from sight.

"Spike!" called his mother.

"Oh No! His sisters screeched from beneath the flowers, "YIKES! THERE HE GOES AGAIN!"

About the Author

Carla Richards is a pseudonym for Trudy Weddington and Stacia Faith, sisters collaborating to write children's books that enhance the imaginations of young readers. One of the authors goals is to teach family values and self-discipline through crafting a fun story.

Trudy Weddington lives in Tulsa, Oklahoma. Having had several articles published in her youth and written other genres, she hopes to continue writing for the benefit of children.

She is married with three grown children and five grandchildren. Trudy enjoys reading several books simultaneously, loves to travel and enjoyed membership in the Society for Creative Anachronism for a number of years.

Other than being a successful writer when she grows up (if she ever does), one of Trudy's goals is to eat chocolate cake decorated with gold at Maxim's in Paris!

Stacia Faith, lives in Houston, Texas, is married with three grown children, and three grandchildren. She is a singer-songwriter, poet, and has written short stories, and screenplay treatments, as well as historic romances.

She is a member of The Society for Children's Books Writers and Illustrators and has received several writing awards as a member of Fort Bend Writer's Guild.

Stacia enjoys reading, writing, and music, and dreams of taking the entire family on a trip around the world!

We'd love to hear from our readers!
Our e-mail address is: Carlarichards1@hotmail.com

Printed in the United States
5987